Teacher's Guide

LEVELED READERS
for Fluency

Grade 1

Columbus, OH

The McGraw·Hill Companies

SRAonline.com

 SRA

The *McGraw-Hill* Companies

Table of Contents

Unit 9 Being Brave

Unit 10 Homes

Leveled Readers for Fluency

The purpose of *Leveled Readers for Fluency* is to promote fluency and accuracy by giving students the opportunity to practice reading at their grade level. Theme-related books at three readability levels—Easy, Average, or Challenge—address the individual needs of all students. Whether used for independent reading or in small, flexible groups, *Leveled Readers for Fluency* builds fluency and strengthens students' reading, vocabulary, and comprehension skills. The controlled content, length, and reading levels of the Readers allow for maximum fluency benefit.

Grade 1 has twenty-four *Leveled Readers.* Two books at each level— Easy, Average, and Challenge— accompany every **Open Court Reading Student Anthology** theme and include fiction and nonfiction selections. The Easy books are written at a kindergarten level; the Average books are written at a first-grade level; and the Challenge books are written at a second-grade level. Each book's readability is easily distinguished by the logo on the back cover:

- ◆ Easy
- ★ Average
- ▲ Challenge

Besides providing fluency practice, each *Leveled Reader* includes vocabulary from the unit to give students extra practice with these words. They are defined at the end of each Reader. Comprehension questions related to one strategy and skill used in the unit are also at the end of each book.

A two-page lesson for each *Leveled Reader* can be found in the *Teacher's Guide.* Each lesson includes a fluency strategy, which covers dialogue, punctuation, headings, or any other element that may interfere with a student's ability to read a selection fluently. In addition to the suggested fluency strategy, vocabulary strategies and definitions are available to support students who need additional help in deciphering the meaning of a word. The *Teacher's Guide* also includes the answers for the comprehension questions.

You can use the *Leveled Readers* in a variety of ways, depending upon the needs of your students. Students can read the books individually to practice reading fluently and accurately, or students can read in pairs. For example, you can pair an accomplished reader with a developing reader, or you can pair two students at the same reading level to read the book to one another. Another strategy might include utilizing small-group choral reading of a particular *Leveled Reader.* Repeated readings of the Readers will help students build fluency as they read and reread familiar text.

Administering Oral Fluency Assessments

Included at the end of each unit in the *Teacher's Guide* are three Oral Fluency Assessments—one Easy, one Average, and one Challenge—and one Scoring Oral Fluency Assessment page. The three assessment passages are taken from the first few pages of a *Leveled Reader.* Choose the fluency assessment that is appropriate for each student, and make two copies. Then make a copy of the Scoring Oral Fluency Assessment page for each student you assess. Cross out the two Oral Reading Accuracy charts on this page that do not apply to the fluency assessment you are administering. If you are unsure of which Oral Fluency Assessment to administer, begin with the Average assessment. If this assessment is too difficult for the student, use the Easy assessment the next time you administer an assessment; if the Average assessment is not difficult enough, give the student the Challenge assessment the next time. Give one copy of the assessment to the student, and keep one copy for yourself.

Have the student sit comfortably at a table with you. Seat yourself and the student so you can mark the Oral Fluency Assessment page unobtrusively without distracting the student. Be sure you also have a pen or pencil, a stopwatch or other timer, and extra paper to record any observations.

Hand the student the fluency assessment, and say that you would like the student to read the passage aloud so you can listen. As you listen, take notes. Tell the student there will not be a grade, so the student will not feel nervous. Tell the student to read the passage carefully and do his or her best. Allow the student a few minutes to look over the text, and then ask whether the student is ready. After making sure the student is ready, tell the student to begin.

Start the timer or watch as the student begins to read. Pronounce any proper nouns with which the student is unfamiliar. Do not count these words as errors. Note: If the student becomes frustrated or makes several consecutive errors, stop the assessment.

At the end of one minute, draw a box around the last word the student reads. If the student is reading with acceptable fluency and you have time available, allow the student to finish the text. As the student reads, draw a line through each word he or she misreads.

The observations you make while the student is reading can be an important source of qualitative data. The observations can inform instruction, identify the student's strengths and weaknesses, and provide information that is not available from traditional quantitative sources.

Scoring Oral Fluency Assessments

The following guidelines will help you score the student's performance accurately:

- If the student makes an error and then self-corrects without your assistance, it should not be counted as an error.
- If the student repeats the same mistake, it should be counted as only one error.
- If the student hesitates for more than five seconds, tell the student the word, and count it as an error.

Scoring Conventions

- Draw a line through any word the student misreads. Count this as an error. If possible, note the type of error (misreading short *a* as short *e*, reading *get* as *jet*, and so on).
- Draw a box around the last word the student reads in one minute.
- Circle words the student omits or refuses to read, and count them as errors, even if you prompt the student.
- Indicate with a caret any extra words the student inserts. If possible, write the inserted word. Count insertions as errors.
- Draw an arrow between words the student reverses. Count these as one error.
- Put two check marks above a word the student repeats. Do not count this as an error.

Finding the Student's Accuracy Rate

Count the total number of words read in one minute. Subtract the number of errors from the total number of words read, and use that figure to find the number of correct words read per minute. If the student has read the entire passage, use the Oral Reading Accuracy chart provided on the Scoring Oral Fluency Assessments page. If not, divide the correct words read per minute by the total number of words to calculate the correct rate. Record these numbers on the Reading Rate and Accuracy chart.

Interpreting Oral Fluency Assessments

First compare the student's number of correct words per minute with the following chart. This will show how the student compares with other students in the same grade at the same time of year. The data in the chart represents the approximate fluency rate a student should attain periodically in the second semester of Grade 1. The two rows of numbers represent the seventy-fifth and the fiftieth percentiles.

	Unit 1	Unit 2	Unit 3	Unit 4	Unit 5	Unit 6	Unit 7	Unit 8	Unit 9	Unit 10	Percentile
Grade 1							47	47	82	82	75
							23	23	53	53	50

Then examine the student's accuracy percentage. Reading accuracy should remain constant or gradually increase within a grade and between grades, until it stabilizes at 90 percent or higher. Compare the student's accuracy percentage after each assessment to ensure his or her accuracy percentage is remaining constant or increasing.

Next examine the types of errors the student is making, and consider how they signify reading behaviors. For example:

- Inserting extra words suggests the student understands what he or she is reading but is reading somewhat impulsively.
- A student who refuses to attempt a word is probably uncertain of his or her abilities and is unwilling to take risks.
- Misreading regular letter sounds implies the student has not yet mastered the conventions of the sound-symbol relationship. This is in contrast with the student who misreads complex letter sounds (alternate sounds, blends, diphthongs, and digraphs) but has little difficulty with regular letter sounds.

Finally consider the error pattern. If errors are scattered randomly throughout the passage, then the error types represent skills the student has not yet developed. If errors increase in frequency from beginning to end, then fatigue or inattention are involved.

Other Considerations

Oral fluency assessments will provide useful information about most students. If a student is reading well below grade level, however, the same fluency assessment can be administered more than once. If the student is making reading progress, his or her accuracy rate should increase.

As a follow-up to the Oral Fluency Assessment, you can use two additional procedures to gain an understanding of the student's comprehension of the passage. One is to ask the student to retell or summarize the passage. Informally evaluate how complete the retelling or summary is. Another is to ask the student typical comprehension questions about the passage, such as "What is this passage mostly about?" or "Why did this happen in the passage?"

Finally it may be useful to establish targets for reading accuracy. These targets may include whether the student reads ten words in a row without errors, whether the student increases the number of correct words read in a minute, or whether the student decreases a specific type of error. Establishing such targets allows you to provide appropriate instructional support and gives the student a goal he or she can achieve in a reasonable amount of time.

Lessons

LEVELED READERS
for Fluency

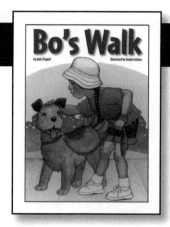

Selection Summary

Mora's dog steps in gum. He tries many ways to get it off.

Number of Words in Leveled Reader: 90

Fluency

Reading in Chunks to Improve Automaticity

- Explain to students that some words are always read together as a small chunk. Turn to page 3 of *Bo's Walk*, and point to the words *the park*. Read the sentence from the book, and model for students what it sounds like to say each word separately. Then tell students to listen to the difference when you repeat the sentence, uttering *the park* as a chunk. Mention to students that small word chunks often begin with words such as *the, a, an, this, these, those, my, your, his, her, our,* and *their*. Explain to students that sometimes number words such as *one* also form a chunk with the word or words that follow. Tell students all these words are clues that the next word or next few words will form a chunk of words that should be read together.

- As a class, look through the book for word chunks that begin with the words *a* and *the*. If time allows, record your list on chart paper or on the board as students identify the individual chunks. Start the list with the word chunk *a red bird*. Read the list together with students. Emphasize reading the words as a chunk.

- Tell students they are going to play the Who Can Find game. Have them work with partners to find chunks of text from *Bo's Walk* that begin with the word *his*. Ask students to list the chunks on a sheet of paper. Have them practice reading these chunks of words. Have students practice reading page 10 aloud, reading the words *his paw* as a chunk.

Vocabulary

spider (page 6) *n.* A small eight-legged animal that spins and lives in a web.
ground (page 7) *n.* The earth; dirt.
paw (page 8) *n.* The foot of an animal, usually with claws.

Comprehension Questions

1. How did you think Bo was going to get the gum off his paw? *(Possible answers: I thought Bo would eat the gum off his paw. I thought Bo would rub the gum off his paw.)*

2. What caused Bo to shake and lick his paw? *(The gum on Bo's paw caused him to shake and lick his paw.)*

3. Why did Bo lift his paw and look at Mora? *(Possible answer: Bo thought Mora could help him take the gum off his paw.)*

 Vocabulary Support

- Write the word *ground* on the board.
- Turn to page 7, and read aloud, "He did not see the gum on the ground."
- Ask students what *ground* means. *("the earth; dirt)*
- As you discuss the meaning of the word, ask students whether *floor* means the same thing as *ground*. Ask whether they can walk across the ground. *(yes)* Ask whether they can walk across a floor. *(yes)* Ask whether they would find the ground inside or outside a building. *(outside)* Ask whether they would find a floor inside or outside a building. *(inside)*
- Write the words *spider* and *paw* on the board. Show students a picture of a spider and a picture of a paw to help them understand these vocabulary words. Ask students to name some animals that have paws. *(Possible answers: dogs, cats, lions)*

 English Learner Tip

Connecting Words and Meanings
Duplicate a picture from *Bo's Walk* that shows Mora and the dog. Underneath the picture, write the terms *the girl* and *the dog*. Partner your English Learner with a more fluent English-speaking student, and have them draw a line from the term to the picture. Then have them say the words multiple times.

Selection Summary

It's fun to use your five senses. Let's try!

Number of Words in Leveled Reader: 92

Fluency

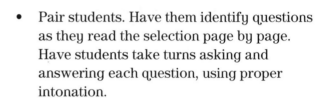

Practicing Intonation by Reading Questions

- Have students look at the sentences on page 5 of *Our Five Senses*. Ask students what they note about the punctuation at the end of the sentences. *(The sentences end with question marks.)* Remind students that people's voices change when they ask a question. Their voices get higher at the end of a question. Discuss with students that a question mark is a special signal that tells how their voices should sound when they read.

- Read aloud the first question on page 5: "Can you see the wind?" Have students silently read the second question: "Can you feel it?" Ask students whether they could hear the question in their minds. Have one student ask the question aloud, and have another student answer it. Tell students to listen closely to how the question and the answer sound. Can they hear a difference? Move on to page 8. Tell students they need to pay careful attention. Ask, "Who wants to read aloud the *question* on page 8?" *(Some students will say the sentence is not a question.)* Ask how the students know it is not a question. *(The sentence does not end with a question mark.)*

- Pair students. Have them identify questions as they read the selection page by page. Have students take turns asking and answering each question, using proper intonation.

Vocabulary

dandelion (page 4) *n.* A plant that has a bright yellow flower.

dew (page 6) *n.* Water droplets that form on grass and go away as the air warms.

thud (page 10) *n.* The sound made when something or someone falls.

Comprehension Questions

1. Name your five senses. *(Possible answer: Our five senses are touching, seeing, hearing, smelling, and tasting.)*

2. What can you see in your classroom? *(Possible answer: I see desks, chalkboards, and pencils.)* What can you hear? *(Possible answer: I hear voices, chairs moving on the floor, and chalk on the chalkboard.)* What can you smell? *(Possible answer: I smell food from the cafeteria and chalk.)* What can you feel? *(Possible answer: I feel smooth paper and cold metal.)* What can you taste? *(Possible answers: I taste my toothpaste from this morning.)*

Vocabulary Support

- Write the word *dandelion* on the board.
- Ask students to find the animal name in the word on the board. *(lion)*
- Explain to students that the word *dandelion* comes from three French words—*dent de lion*—that mean "lion's tooth."
- Display a picture of a dandelion with its leaves.
- Have students observe the leaves and tell how they could resemble lion teeth.
- Write the word *dew* on the board.
- Show students a picture of *dew* on a leaf or on grass.
- Ask students whether they ever walk in grass early in the morning. Lead them to realize that grass is sometimes wet in the morning. Explain to them that the wetness is dew.

English Learner Tip

Format of a Question Talk to Spanish-speaking students about questions. Have students describe what a question looks like when it is written in Spanish. In Spanish text, an upside-down question mark (¿) is at the beginning of the question, and a standard question mark (?) is at the end of the question. Help students remember that in English text, a question has only one question mark, which appears at the end of the question.

Indoor Recess
by Ashon Lewis
illustrated by Diane Paterson

Selection Summary
It is raining outside, but the class wants to have recess. What will they do?

Number of Words in Leveled Reader: 191

Fluency

Reading Descriptive Words with Expression

- Explain to students that some words are used to make you feel a certain way. Tell them the *way* you read words is as important as the words you use.

- Ask students to listen to the way you read a sentence from *Indoor Recess*. Then, with dramatic expression, read the first sentence on page 3: "It was a *cold, wet day.*" Ask students how hearing the sentence made them feel. Reread the sentence, but this time read it quickly and cheerfully. Ask students to describe the difference between the first time and the second time you read the sentence. *(The first read sounded sad and depressing. The second read was confusing because it sounded happy.)* Tell students the author is trying to describe the bad weather with words, but remind students that the way they read the words is important too.

- Reread the story with the class. After reading each sentence, have students echo read it, mimicking your expression as they read.

Vocabulary

thud (page 3) *n.* The sound made when something or someone falls.
awful (page 3) *adj.* Bad or unpleasant.
shout (page 5) *v.* To call loudly; to yell.

Comprehension Questions

1. How did you clarify difficult words or ideas? *(Possible answers: I clarified difficult words by listening to how the teacher read the story. I clarified difficult ideas by thinking about how I would feel if I were one of the students in the classroom.)*

2. How was the class problem solved? *(The class problem was solved by studets' voting for games they wanted to play inside.)*

Vocabulary Support

- Write the word *thud* on the board.
- Tell the class to listen as you drop a book flat on the floor. Ask students to describe the sound.
- Tell students the word *thud* imitates the sound the book made as it hit the floor. Drop the book again, and say "thud."
- Reread the first two sentences on page 3. Tell students to remember the sound the book made as it hit the ground as you read the word *thud*.
- Write the word *awful* on the board.
- Ask students to provide reasons people might dislike the weather in the story. *(scary noises; can't play outside; cold; get wet going from one place to another)*
- Ask students to describe how they would feel if they were outside in the weather described in the story. *(cold; wet; sad; horrible; tired; sick)*
- Tell students the author used the word *awful* to show the weather was bad and unpleasant.

English Learner Tip

Understanding Cultural Gestures Some physical gestures are unique to a culture. Help students understand that putting one's finger to one's lips is a way of asking people to be quiet.

Selection Summary
Read the clues. Guess each animal!

Number of Words in Leveled Reader: 182

Fluency

Practicing Intonation by Reading Questions

- Remind students that people use different voices when asking a question and giving an answer. People's voices rise at the end of a question—in fact, the rise in pitch is a clue that someone is asking a question.

- Model read questions for students by reading the question on page 3. Then say the sentence "I have a dog." Point out to students that this sounds like a true statement. Now ask the question "I have a dog?" Tell students you said the exact same words but you said them in a different way. Have students describe the difference.

- Tell students they are going to play the Question and Answer game. Write on separate cards the questions that appear on pages 3, 5, 7, and 9 of *Animal Clues*, and write on separate cards the answers to those questions (on pages 4, 6, 8, and 10). Organize students into four groups. Give each group one question card and one answer card. Let the groups take turns reading chorally their questions and answers.

Vocabulary

spider (page 6) *n.* A small eight-legged animal that spins and lives in a web.
thirsty (page 7) *adj.* Needing a drink.

Comprehension Questions

1. What did you visualize as you read the clues? *(Possible answers: I visualized the animals that were being described. I visualized the animal I thought was being described.)*

2. Describe details about each of the animals in the book. *(Possible answers: The dog looks fast and furry. The spider has many eyes. The elephant has small eyes and thick eyelashes. The ostrich has funny-looking feet and lots of feathers.)*

 Vocabulary Support

- Say the word *thirsty*, and write it on the board.
- Tell students *thirsty* contains a hidden word.
- If students cannot guess the word *thirst*, tell them the word. In either case, underline that part of the word. *(thirsty)*
- Explain that you can say someone *has a thirst* or that someone *is thirsty*. Both mean the same thing.
- Have students pantomime how they might tell someone they are thirsty.
- Ask students to think of all the spider songs and stories they know. Write the heading Spiders on the board, and then write the class's list beneath it. *(Possible answers: Itsy Bitsy Spider, Little Miss Muffet, Charlotte's Web, The Very Busy Spider, Be Nice to Spiders)*

 English Learner Tip

Practicing and Sharing Working with a partner, English Learners can quickly learn common animal words such as *dog* and *elephant*. Encourage English Learners to share some of their culture by saying the name of each animal in the reader in English and in their native language.

Selection Summary

Sam loves baseball, but he is not very good at it. After a lot of practice, that changes.

Number of Words in Leveled Reader: 409

Fluency

Using Expression in Reader's Theater

- Expression is an important skill for building fluency. One way to improve expression is to have students practice for a reader's theater performance of the text. Reader's theater is an oral presentation of text. For a reader's theater, students use the text to create a script they will read aloud. As students practice, or rehearse, for their performances, they grow more comfortable with the text and have opportunities to demonstrate expression in their roles. Reader's theater does not require costumes, props, or a set. Students should read from the script or from the reader during the reader's theater.

- Before you begin the reader's theater, turn to page 4 in *Sam at Bat*. Tell students that in order to read with expression, they should first imagine how a character is feeling. Have students look at Sam and imagine how he is feeling. Have them do the same for Sam's mother and Sam's brother. Then read the page aloud, modeling expression. Have students listen for expression as you read.

- Organize the class into groups of four. Assign students to the roles of Sam, Sam's mother, Nate, and Narrator. Have each student practice reading their script or lines with expression. Offer encouragement and feedback about expression as students practice their roles. Provide time for each group to present its performance.

Vocabulary

awful (page 4) *adj.* Bad or unpleasant.
ground (page 9) *n.* The earth; dirt.
thud (page 9) *n.* The sound made when something or someone falls.

Comprehension Questions

1. What questions did you ask yourself as you read the story? *(Possible answers: During the story, I asked myself whether Sam would ever get better. During the story, I asked myself whether Nate would get tired of helping Sam. During the story, I asked myself whether Sam would stick with it or if he would give up.)*

2. What happened in the beginning of the story, in the middle, and in the end? *(Possible answer: The story started with Sam being sad that he was not very good at baseball. In the middle of the story, Sam practiced and worked hard. At the end of the story, Sam's hard work made him a better baseball player.)*

Vocabulary Support

- Write the word *ground* on the board.
- Read from page 9 of *Sam at Bat* "Some of the balls hit the ground . . ." Ask students what *ground* means.
- Write *playground* on the board. Ask students what two words make the word *playground* and what the word means. *(play, ground; "an outdoor area for children to play in)*
- Tell students England has a train called the Underground. Have them guess why it has that name. *(The train goes under the ground.)*
- Write the word *thud* on the board.
- Ask a student to drop a book gently, and tell the class to listen to the sound the book makes when it hits the floor. Discuss with students that the word *thud* imitates the sound of the book hitting the floor. Ask students to suggest at least three examples of things that thud—for instance, a shoe falling on the floor, a tennis ball hitting a wall, and the sound of feet jumping on the floor.

Dogs to the **Rescue!**
by Nick Grant

Selection Summary

Rescue dogs are special dogs. They help find people who are missing or trapped.

Number of Words in Leveled Reader: 394

Fluency

Reading in Chunks for Automaticity

- Copy the text from page 4 of *Dogs to the Rescue!* on the board or on chart paper. Read the sentences aloud. Have students note the different lengths of the sentences. Then talk about the importance of reading groups of words together, or in chunks. Explain that a chunk is a group of words read together to help them understand the meaning of a sentence. To demonstrate reading in chunks, read the first sentence, and underline the chunks *Many rescue workers* and *help these people.* Now read the second sentence, and underline all three words: *The police help.* Lead students to see that sometimes a sentence can be made of several chunks, and sometimes a sentence can be an entire chunk by itself.

- Review the remaining sentences you have written, asking the students to decide which chunks to underline. Read aloud—or ask a student to read aloud—each sentence, reading the chunks together.

- Have students work in small groups. Each group should work on a different page of the book to decide how to break the sentences into chunks. If an entire page seems too much, assign a sentence to each group. Allow students to copy the sentences themselves, or distribute handouts you have made. As you walk from group to group to answer questions and offer guidance, say aloud the sentences students are writing so they can hear the chunks they are choosing. When students have completed their task, have them read their sentences to each other or to another group.

Vocabulary

awful (page 3) *adj.* Bad or unpleasant.
frightened (page 11) *adj.* Afraid; scared.
thirsty (page 13) *adj.* Needing a drink.

Comprehension Questions

1. Summarize the selection. *(Possible answer: Dogs are smart and helpful animals. Trainers take care of the dogs and teach them how to help people.)*

2. Why are rescue dogs special? *(Possible answer: Rescue dogs are special because they are brave, fast, smart, and strong. Dogs can find things people can't because they have a good sense of smell.)*

 ## Vocabulary Support

- Write the words *frightened* and *frighten* on the board.
- Remind students they are learning about past-tense verbs in this Keep Trying unit. Ask students how the two words look different. *(One ends in -ed.)* Tell students the *-ed* ending shows *frightened* is a past-tense verb.
- Read the following sentence: "I hope it doesn't thunder, because loud noises _____ my dog." Ask students whether loud noises still scare the dog or whether the dog was scared only in the past. Ask them which word they should use to fill the blank. *(frighten)* Next read: "The baby was _____ by the noisy dog." Ask students which word they should use. *(frightened)* Remind students the word *was* tells them to use a past-tense verb.
- Write the word *thirsty,* and ask students what kinds of things make them feel like they need a drink. *(Possible answers: eating salty or hot foods, being in the hot sun, running, playing sports)*

 ## English Learner Tip

Pronouncing /i/ Spelled *i* Native speakers of Spanish and some other languages may pronounce *i* like the vowel sound in *feet.* Provide English Learners with extra practice associating *i* with the /i/ sound in English words such as *pit, pill, him,* and *tin.*

Name _____ Date _____

Oral Fluency Assessment

Unit 7, Fiction ◆

Read the selection *Bo's Walk* accurately and clearly in one minute.

Bo's Walk, pages 3–11

One morning Mora walked Bo to the	1–7
park.	8
Bo was so happy. His tail wagged and	9–16
wagged.	17
Bo saw a red bird in a tall tree.	18–26
Bo saw a tiny spider on an orange flower.	27–35
He did not see the gum on the ground.	36–44
Bo shook his paw. The gum would not	45–52
come off.	53–54
He licked his paw. The gum would not	55–62
come off.	63–64
Bo lifted his paw and looked at Mora. She	65–73
looked closely at his paw.	74–78
"Silly dog," laughed Mora. Then she pulled	79–85
the gum off Bo's paw.	86–90

Unit 7 • Leveled Readers for Fluency

Name _____ Date _____

Oral Fluency Assessment

Unit 7, Fiction ★

Read the following passage from *Indoor Recess* accurately and clearly in one minute.

Indoor Recess, pages 3–7

It was a cold, wet day. The rain hit the	1–10
window with a thud. Lightning flashed outside	11–17
the classroom window. It was an awful day.	18–25
It was time for recess, and the children	26–33
were not happy. They wanted to go outside	34–41
and play.	42–43
"What can we do inside?" asked Juan.	44–50
Maya shouted her idea. "I want to paint!"	51–58
Ryan shouted his idea. "I want to play tag!"	59–67
Everyone started talking. The room got	68–73
very noisy. It got too noisy!	74–79
Miss Gray stood up and covered her ears.	80–87
"Let's try to agree! We'll take a vote!" she	88–96
exclaimed.	97

Name _____ Date _____

Oral Fluency Assessment

Unit 7, Fiction ▲

Read the following passage from *Sam at Bat* accurately and clearly in one minute.

Sam at Bat, pages 3–6

Sam loved baseball. He went to all his	1–8
brother's baseball games. He watched	9–13
baseball on television. Sam wanted to be a	14–21
good baseball player like his brother.	22–27
"Why don't you try out for the school	28–35
team, Sam?" asked his mother.	36–40
Sam shook his head. "All I got to do last	41–50
year was sit on that awful bench," Sam	51–58
replied.	59
Sam's brother, Nate, was listening. "I'll	60–65
help you, Sam," he said. "If you practice,	66–73
you'll get better!"	74–76
Sam shook his head. Then he saw his	77–84
baseball glove in the corner. "Well, maybe if	85–92
I practice, I could be good."	93–98

Scoring Oral Fluency Assessments

If the student reads the entire passage in one minute, use the appropriate Oral Reading Accuracy chart to identify the student's score.

Unit 7, Fiction ◆
Bo's Walk,
pages 3–11

Unit 7, Fiction ★
Indoor Recess,
pages 3–7

Unit 7, Fiction ▲
Sam at Bat,
pages 3–6

Oral Reading Accuracy Number of Words = 90	
# of Errors	% Score
1	99
2	98
3	97
4	96
5	94
6	93
7	92
8	91
9	90

Oral Reading Accuracy Number of Words = 97	
# of Errors	% Score
1	99
2	98
3	97
4	96
5	95
6	94
7	93
8	92
9	91
10	90

Oral Reading Accuracy Number of Words = 98	
# of Errors	% Score
1	99
2	98
3	97
4	96
5	95
6	94
7	93
8	92
9	91
10	90

If the student does not read the entire passage, divide the Number of Correct Words Read Per Minute (WPM) by the Total Words Read to determine the student's score. Record these numbers on the Reading Rate and Accuracy chart.

Reading Rate and Accuracy	
Total Words Read:	_____
Number of Errors:	− _____
Number of Correct Words Read Per Minute (WPM):	_____
Accuracy Rate: (WPM ÷ Total Words Read)	_____

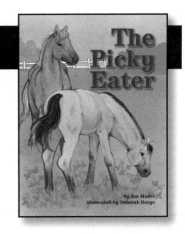

Selection Summary

Tonk is a colt. He is a picky eater. His mother plays a game to get him to eat.

Number of Words in Leveled Reader: 103

Fluency

Using Periods and Pitch to Practice Intonation

- Write the first sentence from page 3 of *The Picky Eater* on the board ("Tonk was lazing in the sun."). Point to the period. Remind students that a period is like a stop sign. The period ends the sentence. Discuss that when people speak to each other, you can hear the end of a sentence. Their voices drop at the end of a sentence. Like the period, the drop in pitch acts as a stop sign. The drop in pitch tells the listener the sentence has ended.

- Tell students that good readers learn to drop their voices at the end of a sentence. Have students listen to your voice as you read the sentence on the board. Model the drop in pitch at the end of the sentence. Have students echo the reading of the sentence multiple times.

- Have each student read one sentence from page 3 or 4. Have students silently read the sentences before they read the sentence aloud. If students are hesitant, have them partner read the sentence.

Vocabulary

laze (page 3) *v.* To relax; to rest.
picky (page 5) *adj.* Hard to please.
nuzzle (page 5) *v.* To gently rub with the nose or snout.

Comprehension Questions

1. How did Tonk's mother get Tonk to eat?
   (Possible answer: Tonk's mother played a game with Tonk. She asked him to try grass. Then she asked him to try clover.)

2. How would you describe Tonk's personality?
   (Possible answer: Tonk has a picky personality. He is hard to please.)

 Vocabulary Support

- Write the word *laze* on the board.
- Ask students what *laze* means. *("to relax or rest")*
- Ask, "What word sounds a lot like *laze* and means 'relaxing' or 'not doing work'?" *(lazy)* "Will a lazy person *laze* around?" *(yes)* "How are the two words alike?" *(They sound alike, and the first three letters are the same.)*
- Explain that the words *nuzzle* and *nose* sound alike. Help students remember the meaning of the word *nuzzle*. Have students picture Tonk gently rubbing his mother with his nose. Have students say the words *nuzzle* and *nose* as they visualize Tonk and his mother.

 English Learner Tip

Echo Reading for Practice Record English Learners as you echo read the story with them. Have students echo after you read each sentence. Then have students listen to the recording as they reread the story multiple times.

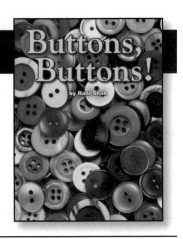

Selection Summary

Look at all the buttons! Let's play with buttons!

Number of Words in Leveled Reader: 91

Fluency

Choral Reading with Expression

- As a class, look at page 3 of the selection. Point to the exclamation points. Explain that an exclamation point tells the reader to read the sentence with excitement.

- Read each sentence on page 3. Model excitement only while reading the first and second sentences. Ask students which sentences sounded exciting. *(the first two sentences)* Ask them how the third sentence sounded. *(like an ordinary statement—no excitement)* Point to the word *biggest* on page 6. Ask students whether they would whisper the word *biggest* or whether they would say it with a strong, loud voice. *(strong and loud)* Tell students to practice their reading with expression. Expression will help them tell the story with the sound of their voice as well as with words.

- This selection lends itself to choral reading. Organize students into small groups, and assign each group different pages so every page will be read. If it is too difficult for groups to read more than one page, assign groups every other page. Read the intervening text yourself. Explain to students that they are going to perform their parts like a poem or song. Have students practice choral reading in their groups. Listen for expression and for pauses between sentences. If students need help, model read the sentence with expression. After groups practice separately, have each group read aloud their sentences. Direct the performance by signaling for a group to begin. Record the performance. Play it back for students, and have them follow along in their readers.

Vocabulary

button (page 3) *n.* A small disk to fasten clothing.
creature (page 10) *n.* A living person or animal.

Comprehension Questions

1. What questions did you ask as you read the selection? *(Possible answers: While I read the selection, I asked where these buttons came from. While I read the selection, I asked what game we were going to play with the buttons.)*

2. Pick two buttons from the selection. How are they alike? How are they different? *(On page 3, two buttons have even-numbered holes. Both buttons are about the same size. One of the buttons looks like a flower. It has two holes. The other button has four holes. It doesn't look like a flower.)*

Vocabulary Support

- Write the word *button* on the board.
- Explain that *button* is an object (as a noun), but button is also an action (as a verb). Hang a shirt with buttons on a hook. Tell a student, "*Button* the shirt." Tell another student, "Point to a *button* on the shirt." Discuss the differences in the use of the word. *(The verb* button *tells what to do with the button; the noun* button *is the object.)*
- Review the definition of *creature.* *("a living person or animal")* Display six pictures—three of animals and three of inanimate objects. Ask students which pictures show creatures and which pictures do not show creatures. Have them explain their answers.

English Learner Tip

Reading and Listening Have English Learners listen to the recording made by the class as they reread the selection.

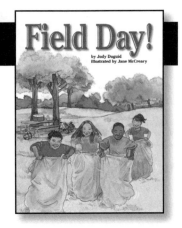

Selection Summary
It's the last day of school, and Becca is happy. Her class is having a field day!

Number of Words in Leveled Reader: 185

Fluency

Progress in Pacing by Pausing at Commas

- Ask students to turn to page 3 of *Field Day!* Write on the board the sentence "The sun was shining, and the birds were singing." Point to the comma. Have students trace the shape of a comma in the air with their fingers. Explain to students that a comma tells readers to pause, or stop for a short time, before they read the next word. Read aloud the sentence on the board. Have students read the word directly after the comma. *(and)*

- Tell students to listen as you read the sentence aloud. Model pausing at the comma. Then have a student read the sentence aloud, making sure to pause at the comma.

- Turn to page 4. Ask students to find the sentence with the comma. Have them silently read the sentence. Then have students read the sentence aloud. Have students read pages 5, 7, and 8 for practice in pausing at commas.

Vocabulary

fourth (page 6) *adj.* Number four in order.

relay race (page 6) *n.* A team race in which each team member takes a turn and completes only one part of the race.

button (page 7) *n.* A small disk to fasten clothing.

giggle (page 11) *v.* To laugh with a short laugh.

Comprehension Questions

1. What happened at the beginning of the story? In the middle? At the end? *(Possible answer: At the beginning of the story, Becca and her class begin field day. In the middle of the story, the teacher can't find the buttons, so the students can't play the game. At the end of the story, Becca finds the buttons.)*

2. How do you visualize the end of the story? What do you see in your mind? *(Possible answer: At the end of the story, I visualize Becca's team winning the button race. I see Becca cheering with her team.)*

Vocabulary Support

- Write the words *first*, *second*, *third*, and *fourth* on the board. Read each word.
- Ask students which word goes with the number *1*, which with *2*, and so on. Write the appropriate number next to the word.
- Organize students into groups of four. Tell each group to form a line. Ask which student is second? First? Fourth? Third? Have students take turns being the fourth person in their line. When groups form new lines, have students count off—*first, second, third, fourth*.
- Tell students that sometimes the word *button* means "a small disk to fasten clothing." Sometimes *button* means something different. What do you push in an elevator to reach a different floor? *(a button)* What do you push on a phone to dial a phone number? *(buttons)* Help them see the resemblance in size and shape among different kinds of buttons.

English Learner Tip

The Sounds /l/ and /r/ Some English Learners may jumble the sounds /l/ and /r/. In many Asian languages, these sounds are considered variations of the same sound. Some students may pronounce the English /r/ as /l/. Allow English Learners time to practice distinguishing the two sounds by reading word pairs such as *lamp, ramp; lace, race; lock, rock;* and *light, right.*

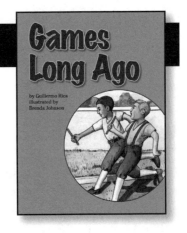

Selection Summary

Children long ago liked to play games. They played some of the same games that children play today.

Number of Words in Leveled Reader: 180

Fluency

Echo Reading to Increase Automaticity

- Ask students whether they know what an echo is. *(sounds or words that are repeated)* Tell students they are going to play the Echo Game, and they are going to be the echoes. Have students silently read the words as you read aloud. Emphasize that as they are reading, they also must listen to *how* you are saying the words. When it is time to be the echo, students must try to read the words with the same expression you used—just as an echo would sound.

- Turn to page 3 of *Games Long Ago*. Have students silently read as you read the first sentence aloud. Choose one student. Read the first sentence in unison with this student. Next have the student echo read the sentence alone.

- Read the last sentence on page 3. Select one student to act as an echo. Continue this exercise with other students and the remaining sentences in the book. If students lack confidence, have them work in pairs to echo read the first two pages. Have these students alternate between being the reader and being the echo.

Vocabulary

relay race (page 6) *n.* A team race in which each team member takes a turn and completes only one part of the race.

laze (page 10) *v.* To relax; to rest.

Comprehension Questions

1. What games did children play long ago? *(Possible answer: Long ago, children played hide-and-seek, hopscotch, marbles, and horseshoes, ran relay races and jumped rope.)*

2. What games do you think children will play in the future? *(Possible answers: In the future, I think children will play the same games. In the future, I think children will play more video games.)*

Vocabulary Support

- Ask students whether they have ever participated in a *relay race*. If so, have them describe the race. If time allows, have students compete in a relay race with erasers or pieces of chalk.
- Explain that people in the Olympics also run relay races. Display pictures of runners in an Olympics relay race.
- Have students think about the word *laze*. Does it make them think of another word they know? *(lazy)* Remind students that *laze* means "to relax or rest." How would they define *lazy*? *(using no energy)* Have students demonstrate "lazing around."

English Learner Tip

Connecting Images to Text Help English Learners understand the games listed in this selection. Provide photos of the games and cards with the names of the games in this selection. Match the names and the photos for students. Have them read the words. Mix the cards, and mix the photos. Have each student select a card and read the name of the game. Then have students match the card with the correct photo. For additional help, allow students to use their reader to match the name and the picture of the game.

Selection Summary

It's the best day of the summer. It's the day of the family picnic!

Number of Words in Leveled Reader: 398

Fluency

Speaker Tags as Cues for Expression in Dialogue

- Turn to page 8 of *Family Fun.* Ask students to identify the quotation marks. Explain that the quotation marks show the dialogue, or the words spoken by the character. Explain that the exclamation point and the word *exclaimed* are clues. These clues tell the reader to read the dialogue in an excited way. They tell how the character feels and how the character will sound when he or she is speaking. Read aloud with expression the sentence containing the dialogue.

- Turn to page 9. Ask a student to point to the quotation marks. Have students run their fingers under the dialogue (the text inside the quotation marks). As a class, read aloud the dialogue. Have students look for clues that tell how Dale should sound. Lead students to the word *shouted* and the exclamation point. Tell them that these are the clues. Ask students how Dale's dialogue should be read. *(loud and with excitement)*

Reread Dale's dialogue, but this time whisper read. Ask, "Did I read the words with the correct expression?" *(no)* Challenge individual students to read the dialogue with proper expression. Ask students to point to the quotation marks on page 15. Have them underline with their fingers the dialogue. Have students point to the expression clues. *(the exclamation point and the word laughed)* Have students read aloud the sentence with proper expression.

- Pair students. Have them partner read the story. Remind students to use the clues to read the dialogue with proper expression.

Vocabulary

picky (page 6) *adj.* Hard to please.
fourth (page 11) *adj.* Number four in order.

Comprehension Questions

1. Which words or phrases did you clarify as you read the story? *(Possible answers: I clarified the word* especially *by reading the rest of the paragraph. I clarified the phrase* Now you're frozen *by looking at the pictures and asking my teacher about the game.)*

2. What was the best part of the day? Why? *(The best part of the day was when the entire family went swimming in the lake. It was the best part because the lake water was cold, and it was hot outside.)*

 Vocabulary Support

- Write the word *picky* on the board. Ask students to name words they can find in *picky. (pick, icky)*
- Discuss with students that both words can fit the definition of *picky*, which means "hard to please." Lead students to see how picky eaters might *pick* only some things out of many to eat. If picky eaters think some foods are *icky*, they will not pick those foods to eat. If time allows, have students work together to write a short poem using the words *picky*, *pick*, and *icky*.
- Review the meaning of *fourth*—"number four in order." Arrange four different-size blocks, from largest to smallest. Ask students to describe the size of the fourth block. *(the smallest)* Change the order of the blocks from smallest to largest. Ask students to describe the size of the fourth block. *(the largest)*

 English Learner Tip

Understanding Concepts Have English Learners turn to pages 8 and 9. The children are playing a game called "freeze tag." Tell students the game is called freeze tag because when a player is tagged, he or she to stay in the same spot without moving, as if frozen. If time allows, have students play a game of freeze tag. Instructions can be found on the Internet.

Selection Summary
Children like to play many games. Some animals like to play some of the same games.

Number of Words in Leveled Reader: 401

Fluency

Recognizing Patterned Repetition to Practice Intonation

- As a class, turn to page 5. Reveal to students the pattern in the book. The pattern begins by describing games children play. The second step of the pattern asks a question. The final part of the pattern describes an animal that plays a game similar to the game played by children. Turn to page 6. Ask students whether the same pattern exists—first, children play a game; second, a question is asked; and finally, animals play a similar game. *(Yes, the same pattern exists.)* Discuss with students that when ideas are repeated, the ideas form a pattern. A pattern helps you know what to expect and how to read the story with proper intonation, or rise and fall of your voice.

- Write the following pattern on the board: *Some children like to _____. Do you like to _____? Animals like to _____.* Have students echo you as you model the intonation of the pattern. Have students follow along as you read pages 5 and 6 from the book *Playing Around.* Have students use the text on page 5 to fill the pattern on the board. Have students do the same for the text on page 6. Prompt students if necessary. Read the completed patterns, and have students echo read with proper intonation.

- Have students work in groups to practice reading the selection, using the same intonation as used in the modeling exercise above.

Vocabulary

giggle (page 3) *n.* A short laugh. *v.* To laugh with a short laugh.
laze (page 15) *v.* To relax; to rest.

Comprehension Questions

1. What is the main idea of the story? *(The main idea of the story is that animals play some of the same games as people.)*

2. Which games in the story do you like to play? *(Possible answer: I like to play like penguins. I like to swim and dive.)*

 Vocabulary Support

- Write on the board and ask students to read the sentence frame "A _____ is a short laugh." Write these words on the board: *wiggle, shoe, pickle, giggle, house, spider, ground,* and *laugh.* Ask students to choose the word that best fits the sentence. *(giggle)* Ask them to explain their answer. Which other word comes close? *(laugh)* Explain that the word *giggle* imitates the sound of a short laugh.
- Have each student finish the sentence with a word that will make them *giggle* when they read the sentence. Have each student read his or her sentence.
- Review with students the meaning of the word *laze*—"to relax; to rest." Ask students to complete the following sentence: "When I laze around, I like to _____." *(Possible answer: read a book)*

Name _____ Date _____

Oral Fluency Assessment

Unit 8, Nonfiction ◆

Read the selection *Buttons, Buttons!*
accurately and clearly in one minute.

Buttons, Buttons! pages 3–11

Buttons, buttons! Look at all the buttons!   1–7
Let's play a game with them.   8–13
   What color are the buttons?   14–18
   What shape are the buttons? Are they   19–25
square? Are they round?   26–29
   Which button is the biggest? Which   30–35
button is the smallest?   36–39
   How many buttons do you see? Do you   40–47
see a few? Do you see many?   48–54
   Which button goes on a jacket?   55–60
   Let's make a clown. Which button would   61–67
make a good nose?   68–71
   Let's make a funny creature. Which   72–77
buttons would make good eyes?   78–82
   Buttons, buttons! Which button do you   83–88
like best? Why?   89–91

Unit 8 • Leveled Readers for Fluency

Name _____ Date _____

Oral Fluency Assessment

Unit 8, Nonfiction ★

Read the following passage from *Games Long Ago* accurately and clearly in one minute.

Games Long Ago, pages 3–8

It is fun to play games in the summer.	1–9
Children long ago liked to play games too.	10–17
What games do you play? What games	18–24
did children play years ago? Did they play	25–32
the same games as you?	33–37
Children long ago played hide-and-seek.	38–44
Do you like to play this game?	45–51
Long ago, children had relay races. They	52–58
had many kinds of relay races. In some	59–66
races they ran as fast as they could.	67–74
In another kind of relay race, children	75–81
used eggs. They carried their eggs on	82–88
spoons. What do you think often happened	89–95
to the eggs?	96–98
Children long ago liked to play hopscotch.	99–105
Have you ever played this game?	106–111

Name _____ Date _____

Oral Fluency Assessment

Unit 8, Nonfiction ▲

Read the following passage from *Playing Around* accurately and clearly in one minute.

Playing Around, pages 3–6

Children like to play many games. They	1–7
like to giggle and have fun. What games do	8–16
you like to play?	17–20
Animals like to play games too. Some	21–27
animals like to play the same games as	28–35
children. Maybe they like to play the same	36–43
games as you!	44–46
Some children like to play catch with a	47–54
beach ball or baseball. Do you like to play	55–63
catch?	64
Dogs like to play catch. Some dogs are	65–72
great leapers. They can jump into the air	73–80
and catch tennis balls or plastic discs.	81–87
Some children like to chase each other.	88–94
Do you like to play chase?	95–100

Scoring Oral Fluency Assessments

If the student reads the entire passage in one minute, use the appropriate Oral Reading Accuracy chart to identify the student's score.

Unit 8, Nonfiction ◆
Buttons, Buttons!
pages 3–11

Unit 8, Nonfiction ★
Games Long Ago,
pages 3–8

Unit 8, Nonfiction ▲
Playing Around,
pages 3–6

Oral Reading Accuracy Number of Words = 91	
# of Errors	% Score
1	99
2	98
3	97
4	96
5	95
6	93
7	92
8	91
9	90

Oral Reading Accuracy Number of Words = 111	
# of Errors	% Score
1	99
2	98
3	97
4	96
5–6	95
7	94
8	93
9	92
10	91
11	90

Oral Reading Accuracy Number of Words = 100	
# of Errors	% Score
1	99
2	98
3	97
4	96
5	95
6	94
7	93
8	92
9	91
10	90

If the student does not read the entire passage, divide the Number of Correct Words Read Per Minute (WPM) by the Total Words Read to determine the student's score. Record these numbers on the Reading Rate and Accuracy chart.

Reading Rate and Accuracy	
Total Words Read:	_____
Number of Errors:	− _____
Number of Correct Words Read Per Minute (WPM):	_____
Accuracy Rate: (WPM ÷ Total Words Read)	_____

Selection Summary

Tasha is sad. She cannot find her teddy bear. A furry friend saves the day.

Number of Words in Leveled Reader: 105

Fluency

Accuracy and Word Order

- Write "had Tasha problem a" on the board. Read the words aloud. Ask students whether the words make sense as they are written.

- Turn to page 3 of *Tasha's Teddy Bear*, and ask students to compare the words in the first sentence, *Tasha had a problem*, with the words on the board. Explain that the words are the same, but the sentence is scrambled. Write the correct sentence under the scrambled one.

- Tell students they are going to play Scrambled Sentences. Have students work with partners or in small groups. Give each group a set of cards that contains the words of a sentence from *Tasha's Teddy Bear*. Each card should have a different word.

- Have students arrange the cards to form a complete, coherent sentence. When each group is finished, ask them to read aloud the sentence. Have students trade sets of cards and play Scrambled Sentences again, using their new cards.

Vocabulary

problem (page 3) *n.* A difficult or uncomfortable situation.

teddy bear (page 3) *n.* A soft, stuffed toy bear.

clever (page 11) *adj.* Smart.

Comprehension Questions

1. Name the toys Tasha has. *(Possible answer: Tasha has dolls, a jump rope, books, and a ball.)* What is her favorite toy? *(Tasha's favorite toy is a teddy bear.)*

2. What is your favorite toy? *(Possible answers: My favorite toy is a ball. My favorite toy is a doll.)*

Vocabulary Support

- Write *problem* on the board. Have students explain Tasha's problem. *(She couldn't find her teddy bear.)* Have students explain how the problem was solved. *(The dog found it.)*
- Provide examples of problems and solutions such as *There is no milk to drink. (problem) Your family buys milk at the store. (solution)* Ask students to make up problem-solution examples. Have a student read his or her problem or solution. Have other students tell whether it is the problem or the solution.
- Display pictures of Teddy Roosevelt. Point to the words *teddy bear* on page 3. Tell students the teddy bear was named after President Teddy Roosevelt. Explain that long ago President Roosevelt was hunting bears. He refused to shoot a helpless bear. People heard the story and began calling their stuffed toy bears *Teddy's* bears.

English Learner Tip

Building Vocabulary Bring in a teddy bear and other toys from the story. Write the names of the toys on one side of a number of cards. Show the cards one at a time to students, and say the word. Have them place the card next to the object it matches. Have them touch the toy and say its name.

A Storm
by Kenneth Ng

Selection Summary

Storms can be scary. The sky gets dark. There are loud noises.

Number of Words in Leveled Reader: 104

Fluency

Echo Reading to Improve Automaticity

- Explain to students that echo reading is repeating a passage after it has been read aloud. Echo reading will help students read expressively and smoothly. Have students listen as you read a passage aloud. Explain that they will reread the passage with the same expression and tone you modeled.

- Have students listen as you read aloud page 3 of *A Storm*. Have students practice an echo read. Encourage students to use appropriate tone and pace. Reread sentences from the selection to model if necessary.

- Reread the last sentence on page 3, and choose a student to act as the echo. Continue this procedure for the entire selection. If students lack confidence, have them work in pairs. Have them alternate reading and being the echo.

Vocabulary

gloomy (page 3) *adj.* Dark.
bang (page 6) *n.* A sudden, loud noise.
exciting (page 11) *adj.* Awesome, very interesting.

Comprehension Questions

1. How does the sky look during a storm? *(Possible answer: The sky looks dark and gloomy during a storm. There may be a flash of lightning.)* How does it look after a storm? *(Possible answer: The sky does not look gloomy. There may be a rainbow.)*

2. How can you predict a storm is coming? *(Possible answers: The sky becomes very dark and gloomy. There is lightning and loud thunder. There is a lot of wind and rain.)*

 ## Vocabulary Support

- Write the word *bang* on the board. Have students review the definition. *("a sudden, loud noise")* Note that *bang* is a word that imitates a sudden, loud sound.
- Ask students to think of things that make a bang, and list them on the board. *(thunder, cannon, drums, a door slamming, backfire, fireworks)*
- Review the definition of *exciting*. *("awesome; very interesting")* Write this list on the board: *birthdays, fireworks, homework, washing clothes, going to an amusement park, sleeping, running in a race.* Ask which events are *exciting* and which events are not exciting. Have students add other examples to the list.

 ## English Learner Tip

Encouraging and Broadening Display a simple picture book with weather scenes and very simple text. Read the book with English Learners, and have them reread the book by themselves. Ask them to summarize each page. Repeat their summaries, adding new words to broaden the explanation and their vocabulary.

Selection Summary

Tomás wants to help the scared dog he finds in his yard.

Number of Words in Leveled Reader: 178

Fluency

Intonation Using Exclamation Points

- Write a big exclamation point on the board. Use two bright colors, one for the dot and the other for the vertical line. Tell students the mark is an exclamation point. When readers see an exclamation point at the end of a sentence, it signals that something exciting is happening. It tells the reader to read the sentence in an exciting way.

- Turn to page 6 of *The Lost Dog.* Point to the exclamation point. Ask students to listen carefully as you read the sentence with proper intonation. Ask students to echo read the sentence as a group. Remind them that their voices should get louder at the end of the sentence.

- Have students read the story to find the next example of an exclamation point. When they identify the example on page 9, ask students to read the sentence. If necessary, model read with proper intonation. Remind students to think of excitement when they see an exclamation point.

Vocabulary

quiver (page 3) *v.* To shake; to tremble; to shiver.

scared (page 8) *adj.* Afraid; frightened; filled with fear.

Comprehension Questions

1. What questions did you ask as you read the story? *(Possible answers: During the story, I asked myself if Tomás would take care of the dog. During the story, I asked myself how Tomás could help the dog. During the story, I asked myself whether Tomás would find the dog's owner.)*

2. Why did Tomás make signs? *(Tomás made signs to find the dog's owner.)*

3. How did the owner find her dog? *(Possible answer: The owner saw Tomás's sign posted in her neighborhood. The sign had information about her lost dog.)*

Vocabulary Support

- Write *quiver* on the board. Tell students that *quiver* is a word they can act out.
- Remind students that *quiver* means "to shake, tremble, or shiver." Model how it looks to quiver as you say the word. Then have students quiver as they repeat the word multiple times.
- Ask students to give an example of something that makes them quiver. Explain that people may quiver when they are scared.
- Write *scared* on the board, and review the definition. Model quivering and looking scared at the same time. Encourage students to do the same.

English Learner Tip

Reinforcing Meaning Display photocopies of the pictures on pages 3 and 4 of *The Lost Dog*. Write the following captions on separate index cards: *The scruffy dog quivered in the backyard. The dog did not see Tomás looking down from his bedroom window.* Have students place each caption under the appropriate picture. Ask students to read the words, or have them echo read with you. Use the pictures to reinforce other words such as *dog, eyes,* and *tail*.

Selection Summary

Some animals make loud noises. The sounds might scare some people.

Number of Words in Leveled Reader: 184

Fluency

Onomatopoeia and Reading with Expression

- Write the heads Animal and Sound side by side on the board. As a class, fill the chart with the animals and the sounds they make. Use animals from *Loud Animals*. *(Animal: lion, hawk, bear, monkey, gray wolf, hyena, elephant; Sound: roar, screech, growl, shout, howl, laugh, trumpet)*

- Read aloud the words *hyena* and *laugh*. Ask students to demonstrate the sound of a laugh. Ask them what comes to mind when they read the words *hyena's laugh. (a loud sound that is funny and scary at the same time)* Read page 9 aloud, modeling expression. Have students do their best impression of a hyena's laugh while saying the word *laugh*. Continue the exercise, using the remaining animals and their sounds.

- Have students work with a partner to read the selection. Make sure the students use expressions that relate to the animals' sounds.

Vocabulary

pleasant (page 9) *adj.* Nice.

excitement (page 9) *n.* A mood or feeling of high interest or energy.

exciting (page 11) *adj.* Awesome; very interesting.

Comprehension Questions

1. Which words did you clarify as you read the story? *(Possible answer: As I read, I clarified the words* aquarium *and* enemy.*)*

2. How do you know whether this story is fantasy or reality? *(Possible answer: I know this story is reality because it gives information about real animals.)*

Vocabulary Support

- Write the words *pleasant* and *exciting* on the board.
- Review the meaning of each word, using appropriate expression. Speak in a calm and positive manner when you say *pleasant*, but use energy and enthusiasm when you say *exciting*.
- Explain that something that is *pleasant* to one person might be more than pleasant to another; it might be *exciting!* For example, some people might think it is pleasant to go on a merry-go-round, whereas others might think it is exciting.
- Have students think of something that is pleasant or exciting. Ask them to share their responses with other students, using appropriate expression when they speak.

English Learner Tip

Connecting Sounds to Written Words
Help English Learners connect the animals' sounds with the words that describe them. If possible, find an Internet site that provides real animal vocalizations. Have students listen to each animal from *Loud Animals.*

The Frightened Mouse
by Ryanne Ronan
illustrated by Rachel Ivanyi

Selection Summary

A little mouse cannot sleep. He is afraid of a big hungry owl.

Number of Words in Leveled Reader: 392

Fluency

Choral Reading to Practice Automaticity

- Have students look at page 9 of *The Frightened Mouse.* Point to the text in italics. Ask what is different about these words. *(The text is slanted.)* Explain that the slanted letters are called italics. Explain that the italics are used to show unspoken dialogue—that the mouse is thinking this question. Model read the dialogue in the sentence. Next have students look at the quotation marks on page 11. Explain that this is also dialogue. The mouse is saying this aloud rather than thinking it. Explain that other books may use quotation marks rather than italics to indicate unspoken dialogue as well as spoken dialogue.

- Organize students into groups of three or four. Have each group practice reading the story together. As you listen to each group read, help students recognize when they should pause. As necessary, join in the reading. Model expression to show fear and other emotions.

- Have students do several rehearsals. When students are ready, audiotape the performance. Make the tape available so students can listen and read aloud with the recording.

Vocabulary

squeal (page 14) *v.* To make a loud, high cry.
excitement (page 14) *n.* A mood or feeling of high interest or energy.
pleasant (page 15) *adj.* Nice.

Comprehension Questions

1. What did you visualize as you read the story? *(Possible answer: As I read the story, I visualized the inside of the mouse's nest.)*

2. Why was the mouse worried? *(Possible answer: The mouse was worried because owls eat mice.)*

Vocabulary Support

- Write the word *squeal* on the board.
- Discuss with students that the word *squeal* sounds like its meaning—"to make a loud, high cry." Discuss the idea that animals can make squealing cries, like the mouse did in *The Frightened Mouse*. Explain that objects such as tires can also make squeals. For example, when a car comes to a fast stop, the tires squeal.
- Write the words *pleasant* and *please* on the board. Ask students to describe how the words are similar.
- Tell students that something that *pleases* them is *pleasant*. Have each student tell something that is pleasant. If time permits, talk about things that are *unpleasant*.

English Learner Tip

Choral Reading Make sure to place English Learners in separate choral reading groups with fluent English speakers. Practicing the choral reading with fluent English speakers will help them form correct fluency skills.

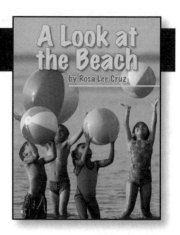

Selection Summary

Many different plants and animals live at the beach. Some people might think they are scary.

Number of Words in Leveled Reader: 403

Fluency

Improve Pacing by Reading in Chunks

- Write on the board the words *above, around, at, below, down, for, from, in, into, of, on, onto, to, under,* and *with.* Tell students to listen for the word *at* as you read. Read aloud the first sentence on page 3 in *A Look at the Beach.* Write the phrase *at the beach* on the board. Explain that good readers read a small group of words (a phrase) together, or in a chunk. These chunks often begin with the words listed on the board. The words listed on the board are clues. They tell the reader that the next few words should be read as a chunk.

- Look at page 4 with students. Ask students to find other examples of clues and chunks. After students identify *for plants and animals,* ask them to read the words as a chunk. Do the same for *from these animals.*

- Have students work with partners or in small groups to identify other chunks in the selection. Have students read and write the phrases. Have them read their completed lists aloud.

Vocabulary

typical (page 6) *adj.* Usual; regular.
tiptoe (page 6) *v.* To walk on one's toes.
excitement (page 12) *n.* A mood or feeling of high interest or energy.
scared (page 14) *adj.* Afraid; frightened; filled with fear.
exciting (page 15) *adj.* Awesome; very interesting.

Comprehension Questions

1. Summarize the selection. *(Possible answer: There are many animals at the beach. It is important to be safe around these animals.)*

2. Describe details about animals that live at the beach. *(Possible answer: At the beach, there are birds with short legs and long wings. There are big sea turtles with flippers. There are crabs that run sideways. At the beach, there are jellyfish that sting and have soft bodies. There is also seaweed that is slimy.)*

 English Learner Tip

Creating a Story Provide old calendars and magazines containing pictures of things you may find at the beach. Have English Learners cut out pictures and paste them onto a large sheet of drawing paper to create a beach scene. Ask students to explain the scene to you. If necessary, describe to them what you see, and have them repeat some of your words.

Vocabulary Support

- Write the words *excitement* and *exciting* on the board. Ask students to identify what is the same about the words. Underline the common letters in each word. *(e, x, c, i, t)*
- Explain that something that is *exciting* gives people a feeling of *excitement*. Give an example of fireworks as something that can be exciting to see and hear. Ask students to name other things that are exciting or that cause excitement. *(Possible answers: riding on a roller coaster, anticipating a birthday party, going on a trip)*
- Ask students what *scared* means. *("afraid; frightened; filled with fear")* Display pictures of a scared person and a happy person. Ask students to identify the picture that shows the scared person. Have them explain their answers. *(Scared people look afraid and unhappy.)*
- Ask students to name things that make people feel scared. *(loud noises, ugly masks)* Explain that everyone feels scared at times. Discuss the idea that some children may be afraid of the dark. Explain that as they get older, they realize there is nothing to be afraid of.
- Ask whether animals can feel scared too. *(yes)* Have students give examples. *(Dogs are often scared of thunder.)*

Oral Fluency Assessment

Unit 9, Fiction ◆

Read the selection *Tasha's Teddy Bear*
accurately and clearly in one minute.

Tasha's Teddy Bear, pages 3–11

Tasha had a problem. She could not find	1–8
her teddy bear.	9–11
Tasha looked and looked for her teddy	12–18
bear.	19
She looked under her bed. Her bear was	20–27
not there.	28–29
Tasha found old shoes and a book. She	30–37
did not find her bear.	38–42
Then Tasha looked in her toy box.	43–49
Tasha found many things. She did not	50–56
find her teddy bear.	57–60
It was getting late. Tasha was tired.	61–67
Buddy ran up to Tasha. He wagged his	68–75
tail. Then he went to the back door and	76–84
barked.	85
Tasha opened the door for Buddy. He	86–92
came back with her teddy bear.	93–98
"You are a clever dog," she laughed.	99–105

Unit 9 • Leveled Readers for Fluency

Name _____ Date _____

Oral Fluency Assessment

Unit 9, Fiction ★

Read the following passage from *The Lost Dog* accurately and clearly in one minute.

The Lost Dog, pages 3–8

The scruffy dog quivered in the backyard.	1–7
It looked forward, and it looked backward,	8–14
but it did not look up.	15–20
The dog did not see Tomás looking down	21–28
from his bedroom window.	29–32
Tomás observed the dog for a while. He	33–40
called his mother to the window. "Do you	41–48
think it has a home?" Tomás asked her.	49–56
"I'm sure it does," Tomás's mother said.	57–63
"We don't need any more pets, so don't	64–71
ask!" she exclaimed.	72–74
That night Tomás heard the trees blowing	75–81
in the wind. Heavy rain fell all night.	82–89
Tomás woke up early the next morning.	90–96

Name _____ Date _____

Oral Fluency Assessment

Unit 9, Fiction ▲

Read the following passage from *The Frightened Mouse* accurately and clearly in one minute.

The Frightened Mouse, pages 3–6

A little mouse made his home under a	1–8
bush. He spent most days looking for food	9–16
and most nights sleeping soundly in his nest.	17–24
One night the mouse had trouble	25–30
sleeping. It started when he peeked out	31–37
of his house to look at the stars. He saw	38–47
something swoop through the air! He did	48–54
not have to take another look. He knew	55–62
what it was. It was an owl and probably	63–71
a hungry one.	72–74
The little mouse had a hard time falling	75–82
asleep that night. He was afraid the owl	83–90
was waiting outside for him. The little	91–97
mouse hid under the covers and waited	98–104
for morning.	105–106

Scoring Oral Fluency Assessments

If the student reads the entire passage in one minute, use the appropriate Oral Reading Accuracy chart to identify the student's score.

Unit 9, Fiction ◆
Tasha's Teddy Bear,
pages 3–11

Unit 9, Fiction ★
The Lost Dog,
pages 3–8

Unit 9, Fiction ▲
The Frightened Mouse,
pages 3–6

Oral Reading Accuracy Number of Words = 105	
# of Errors	% Score
1	99
2	98
3	97
4	96
5	95
6	94
7	93
8	92
9	91
10–11	90

Oral Reading Accuracy Number of Words = 96	
# of Errors	% Score
1	99
2	98
3	97
4	96
5	95
6	94
7	93
8	92
9	91
10	90

Oral Reading Accuracy Number of Words = 106	
# of Errors	% Score
1	99
2	98
3	97
4	96
5	95
6	94
7	93
8–9	92
10	91
11	90

If the student does not read the entire passage, divide the Number of Correct Words Read Per Minute (WPM) by the Total Words Read to determine the student's score. Record these numbers on the Reading Rate and Accuracy chart.

Reading Rate and Accuracy	
Total Words Read:	_____
Number of Errors:	– _____
Number of Correct Words Read Per Minute (WPM):	_____
Accuracy Rate: (WPM ÷ Total Words Read)	_____

Selection Summary

A fuzzy squirrel moves to a new home. It is by the pond.

Number of Words in Leveled Reader: 105

Fluency

Rereading to Improve Accuracy

- Explain to students that reading a story multiple times helps readers become fluent readers. Tell them the more they reread stories, the more natural their reading will sound. Multiple readings will help students read quickly, expressively, and smoothly.

- Model reading page 3 of *A Good Home* at a slow pace to the students. Continue rereading *A Good Home* at a comfortable rate, lowering and raising your voice throughout the story. Stop at the end of each sentence, and pause for commas.

- Have students reread *A Good Home.* They should read with appropriate speed and voice pitch. Listen to individual students read, and record their progress.

Vocabulary

sometimes (page 4) *adv.* At times; part of the time.

until (page 6) *prep.* Up to a certain time or place.

protect (page 10) *v.* To keep safe.

Comprehension Questions

1. Visualize the squirrel back in her old nest. What do you see? *(Possible answers: I see a tiny gray squirrel with a long bushy tail and thick fur. It has large cute eyes and sharp claws. The squirrel is sitting in her nest in the oak tree.)*

2. How do you know this story is a fantasy? *(Possible answer: This is a fantasy because squirrels can't talk. Squirrels do not have hands.)*

 Vocabulary Support

- Write *sometimes* on the board. Ask students which two words make the word. *(some and times)*
- Ask students whether *sometimes* means "something that happens *all* the time," "something that happens *part* of the time," or "something that *never* happens." *("something that happens part of the time")* Explain that the word *some* is the clue.
- Write the word *until* on the board, and review the meaning with students. *("up to a certain time or place")* Model how to use *until* in a sentence. *(I will keep jumping until I have jumped ten times.)* Write the beginnings of sentences such as "I will be very quiet until ____" or "The dog ran until ____" on strips of paper. Distribute the strips to students, and ask them to tell how they would complete the sentences.

 English Learner Tip

Visualization Allow students who have difficulty expressing themselves orally to draw pictures of their visualizations. Encourage them to use words to describe their drawings.

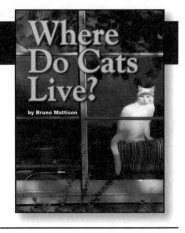

Selection Summary
Cats live and sleep in many places.

Number of Words in Leveled Reader: 102

Fluency

Intonation and Pausing at the End of a Sentence

- Explain to students that periods let readers know they should pause. Periods tell readers the sentence is a statement. Tell students a period is like a stop sign. It shows that the sentence ends. Tell students that when people speak to each other, the drop in their voices indicates when a sentence ends. Like the period, the drop in pitch acts as a stop sign, telling the listener the sentence has ended.

- Tell students that good readers learn to pause at the end of a sentence. Ask students to listen as you read page 3 of *Where Do Cats Live?* Carefully model the correct pace and pitch.

- Call on students to read the sentences on pages 4 and 5. If a recording device is available, let students record and then listen to themselves. Remind them to use the appropriate pitch at the end of each sentence.

Vocabulary

where (page 3) *adv.* In what place; in what location.

porch (page 7) *n.* A covered entrance on the back or front of a house.

sometimes (page 11) *adv.* At times; part of the time.

Comprehension Questions

1. Which words did you clarify as you read the story? *(Possible answer: I didn't know what a vet's office was. I clarified it by reading carefully and looking at the picture. I realized the word* vet *means "a veterinarian.")*

2. Do all cats sleep on laps? *(Possible answers: No. Cats sleep in many different places. Some cats sleep on chairs or on beds in apartments or houses. Cats might sleep in a barn on a farm. Some might sleep by a window at the vet's office.)*

Vocabulary Support

- Write *where* on the board, and review its meaning. *("in what place"; "in what location")* Have students look at the title of the story *Where Do Cats Live?* and note that *where* is often part of a question.
- Write *there* next to *where*, and have students note the similarities between the two words. *(They look alike and rhyme.)* Tell students they can think of the words almost as a pair. One asks the question, and the other answers it. For example, *"Where is the book? It is over there."*
- Discuss the word *porch*. Explain that a porch is a covered entrance to a house that usually has a separate roof. Present pictures of porches, and help students note that porches can be small front porches or big wraparound porches.

English Learner Tip

Vocabulary Have students draw pictures and write a sentence about the different places cats might sleep. Provide students with sentence frames to complete. For example:
Some cats live _____. They sleep _____.
Make sure the pictures match the sentences.

Selection Summary

A robin wants to make a pretty nest. She wants it to sparkle and shine.

Number of Words in Leveled Reader: 212

Fluency

Partner Reading to Enhance Accuracy

- Explain to students that as readers, their job is to read with accuracy. Accuracy means to read words correctly, pausing at the correct time and reading with correct pronunciation. Tell them that by reading the selection multiple times, they will improve their accuracy.

- Turn to page 3 of *The Greedy Robin,* and ask students to follow along as you model reading the text aloud. Ask students to point out any difficult words. Say these words aloud, and have students repeat them.

- Explain to students that they are going to work with a partner to read *The Greedy Robin.* Pair students, and select facing pages for them to read. Tell them they will practice reading their parts twice. The first time, one partner will read the page aloud as the second partner reads along quietly. The next time, the second partner will read aloud as the first partner reads along quietly. If time allows, the partners can choose another set of facing pages and repeat the process.

Vocabulary

build (page 3) *v.* To put together or form.
shelter (page 4) *n.* A place of protection from danger or weather.

Comprehension Questions

1. How would you summarize the story? *(Possible answer: A greedy robin wanted to build a nest that sparkled. Each time she found shiny materials, she was in danger. She finally decided to build a regular nest for shelter.)*

2. How was the nest the greedy robin built different from the one she planned to build? *(The robin planned to build a pretty nest that sparkled. She built a nest from grass, twigs, and mud.)*

 Vocabulary Support

- Write the word *build* on the board, and ask students what it means. *("to put together or form")* Ask a student to read the sentence on page 3 of *The Greedy Robin*. What is the robin going to build? *(a nest)*
- Turn to page 11, and ask a student to read the first sentence. Then write the word *built* next to *build*. Ask students what the difference in meaning is between the two words. *(One indicates the present, and the other indicates the past.)*
- Write *shelter* on the board. Ask students what *shelter* means. *("a place of protection from danger or weather")* Ask students to think of different kinds of shelter. *(trees, bus shelters, nests, houses)* List answers on the board, and ask students to explain their answers.

 English Learner Tip

Monitoring and Clarifying When English Learners encounter a confusing word or passage in the story *The Greedy Robin*, use pictures, objects, stick drawings, or pantomime to help them understand the meaning of the word or passage.

BAT HOMES

BY IAN WILLIAMS

Selection Summary
Bats live in many kinds of homes.

Number of Words in Leveled Reader: 181

Fluency

Using Action Verbs to Determine Intonation

- Discuss with students the idea that some action words (action verbs and verb phrases) are special reading clues. They tell readers how to express the meaning of the sentence by doing what the words say. Words such as *whisper, shout, sleep, run fast,* and *walk slowly* tell the reader to speak in a soft or loud voice. Readers may change their pitch and stress certain action words.

- Model reading the first sentence on page 4 of *Bat Homes*. First read the sentence with no expression. As you reread the sentence, speak softly as you read the action word *sleep*. Ask students which read sounds better. Turn to page 7, and read the first sentence. Be sure to stress the word *scared*.

- Have students read the first sentence on page 7. Ask them to read the sentence aloud to a partner. Encourage students to change the pitch of their voices as they read action words.

Vocabulary

first (page 7) *adj.* Being ahead of all others; being in the front or beginning.
sometimes (page 9) *adv.* At times; part of the time.
own (page 10) *adj.* Belonging to oneself.
build (page 10) *v.* To put together or form.

Comprehension Questions

1. Have you ever seen a bat? Have you seen any bat homes? *(Possible answer: I have seen a bat flying in the sky. It was black with long narrow wings. I have seen bats living in trees, caves, and under bridges.)*

2. Name the different places bats live. *(Possible answer: Bats can live in trees, in caves, and under bridges.)*

English Learner Tip

Vocabulary Provide five different-colored blocks, and have English Learners work with a partner. Put ten folded clues into a bowl. The clues should say things such as "Put the yellow block first," "Put the red block second," or "Put the yellow block fifth." Have partners take turns choosing a clue and moving the block to the position the clue specifies.

Vocabulary Support

- Write the word *first* on the board, and ask what it can mean. *("the number one" or "a person who wins a race")* Ask students to read page 7 of *Bat Homes*, and ask what *first* means in this instance. *("in the beginning")*
- Point to the sentence on page 8 that starts with the word *Then*. Explain that *first* is often followed by the word *then, second,* or *next*—but *first* always comes first.
- Write *sometimes* on the board. Ask students what two words make the word. *(some* and *times)* Ask students whether *sometimes* means "something that happens *all* the time," "something that happens *part* of the time," or "something that *never* happens." *("something that happens part of the time")* Explain that the word *some* is the clue.
- Read the first sentence on page 10, and discuss the use of *own*. Note that people and animals can have their own homes. People can also have their own thoughts or say something in their own words. With the students' help, make a class list of pronouns that can be used with *own*. *(my own, his own, her own, its own, your own, our own, their own)* Ask students to suggest sentences using each phrase from the list. *(I have my own room. My brother has his own bicycle.)*

From the City to the Country

by J. P. Kelly
illustrated by Jennifer Emery

Selection Summary

Abby and her grandma are moving. Abby does not think she will like her new house.

Number of Words in Leveled Reader: 386

Fluency

Intonation Using Exclamation Points

- Write a big exclamation point on the board using two bright colors of chalk or markers, one for the dot and the other for the vertical line. Explain to students that the mark is an exclamation point. An exclamation point at the end of a sentence signals that something exciting has happened. The exclamation point tells readers to say the end of the sentence with feeling and excitement.

- Turn to page 3 of *From the City to the Country* to show students the exclamation point. Then ask students to listen carefully as you read the sentence with feeling. Have them note that your voice gets a little louder at the end of the sentence. Point out that the sentence with the exclamation point is dialogue, and you are trying to make it sound the way Abby would speak it.

- Have students practice reading the sentence with feeling. Encourage those who don't succeed to try again, and remind them to think of excitement when they see an exclamation point.

Vocabulary

porch (page 3) *n.* A covered entrance on the back or front of a house.

where (page 6) *adv.* In what place; in what location.

above (page 11) *prep.* Over; on top of.

sometimes (page 14) *adv.* At times; part of the time.

Comprehension Questions

1. Do you predict that Abby will like her new house in the country? *(Possible answer: I predict Abby will like her new house in the country. I think she will like playing with the ducks and enjoy the farmhouse. I predict she will make new friends.)*

2. What caused Abby to change her mind about her new house? *(Possible answer: When she actually saw the house, Abby liked the big trees, wooden fences, and wide porch. She liked the ducks that were walking across the yard.)*

 English Learner Tip

Practicing Direction Words Print on each side of a strip of cardboard the opposite words *over* and *under,* one word on each side of the strip. Do the same for the words *above* and *below, top* and *bottom,* and *up* and *down.* Review the meaning of each word. Play Simon Says, using the direction words.

 Vocabulary Support

- Write *where* on the board. Explain to students that *where* is a question word. Discuss the type of information that answers the question word. Write *there* next to *where,* and have students note the resemblance between the two words. *(They look alike and rhyme.)* Tell them they can think of the words almost as a pair. One asks the question, and the other answers it. For example, "*Where* is the book? It's over *there.*"

- Write the word *above* on the board. Explain that it means "over" or "on top of." Explain that *above* is a direction word. It tells the location of something. Explain that sometimes the word *above* can answer a question that starts with *where.* Tell students to read the text on page 11. Ask, "*Where* was the sign that read 'Wildflower Farm'?" (above *the gate*)

- Write *sometimes* on the board. Ask students what two words make the word. (*some* and *times*) Ask students whether *sometimes* means "something that happens *all* the time," "something that happens *part* of the time," or "something that *never* happens." ("*something that happens* part *of the time*") Explain that the word *some* is the clue.

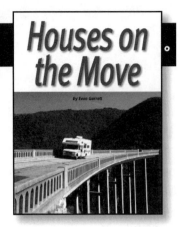

Selection Summary
People live in many kinds of homes. Some homes can be easily moved.

Number of Words in Leveled Reader: 392

Fluency

Pausing after Punctuation Marks to Improve Pacing

- Review with students the punctuation marks *comma, period, question mark,* and *exclamation point.* Explain that each of these marks is a signal to pause after the mark. Pausing gives the reader (and the listener) time to understand what the sentence means.

- Turn to page 6 of *Houses on the Move,* and direct students' attention to the comma in the second sentence. Model reading the second sentence on page 6, pausing after the comma. Ask students whether they could hear the pause. Turn to page 8, and model reading the first two sentences. Ask students to listen for the pause between sentences.

- Have students read the sentences on page 6. Ask them to practice reading the sentences to themselves silently. Then have them say the sentences aloud to a partner.

Vocabulary

shelter (page 4) *n.* A place of protection from danger or weather.

until (page 12) *prep.* Up to a certain time or place.

sometimes (page 13) *adv.* At times; part of the time.

first (page 14) *adj.* Being ahead of all others; being in the front or beginning.

Comprehension Questions

1. What questions did you ask as you read the story? *(Possible answers: As I read the story, I asked myself which houses were easy to move. I asked myself how people moved houses. I wondered how the houses looked after they were moved.)*

2. Which houses can people easily move? *(People can easily move motor homes, houseboats, and tents.)*

 English Learner Tip

Phonics Spanish, Tagalog, Vietnamese, and some other languages lack the /sh/ sound, as in *shelter*. Students may say /ch/ in place of /sh/. For native speakers of such languages, demonstrate how to make the /sh/ sound, and provide additional practice using other /sh/ words.

 **Vocabulary Support**

- Write *shelter* on the board. Review with students what *shelter* means. *("a place of protection from danger or weather")* Ask students to think of the different kinds of shelters described in the book. *(motor homes, houseboats, tents, houses)* Ask students whether an igloo can be a shelter. *(yes)* Have them describe other shelters. *(trees, bus shelters, nests, apartments)* List their answers on the board, and ask students to explain them.

- Write the word *until* on the board, and review its meaning with students. *("up to a certain time or place")* Give an example such as "I will keep walking *until* I have walked for forty-five minutes." Then write the beginnings of sentences such as "I will not eat dinner until _____" or "The children played until _____" on strips of paper. Distribute the strips to students, and ask them which words they would use to complete the sentences.

- Give students strips of paper printed with the words *first, next, then,* and *last.* Have students go to the front of the room, holding their signs so their classmates can read them. Ask students to line up in the correct order according to their signs. Discuss the idea that *first* and *last* always have to be in a certain place, but *next* and *then* have no special order.

Name _____ Date _____

Oral Fluency Assessment

Unit 10, Nonfiction ◆

Read the selection *Where Do Cats Live?*
accurately and clearly in one minute.

Where Do Cats Live? pages 3–11

Where do cats live? They live and sleep	1–8
in many places.	9–11
Some cats live in houses or apartments.	12–18
They may sleep on chairs. They may sleep	19–26
on beds.	27–28
Some cats live on farms. They may live	29–36
with many animals.	37–39
They may sleep in a barn. They may sleep	40–48
on a porch.	49–51
Some cats live outside. They may sleep	52–58
on the ground. They may sleep on a step.	59–67
Some cats live at the vet's office or in a	68–77
store. They may sleep by the window.	78–84
Cats live and sleep in many places.	85–91
Sometimes, no matter where they live,	92–97
many cats sleep on laps.	98–102

Name _____ Date _____

Oral Fluency Assessment

Unit 10, Nonfiction ★

Read the following passage from *Bat Homes* accurately and clearly in one minute.

Bat Homes, pages 3–7

Bats live throughout the world. They live	1–7
in many different kinds of homes.	8–13
Bats sleep in their homes during the day.	14–21
When they sleep, they hang upside down	22–28
with their wings folded. At night they fly out	29–37
to get food. Most bats like to eat insects.	38–46
Many bats live in caves. Most caves are	47–54
very dark inside, but these caves are not	55–62
too dark for bats.	63–66
Some bats live under bridges. Austin,	67–72
Texas, has a big bridge. Many bats live	73–80
under it.	81–82
At first people in Austin were scared of	83–90
the bats. They did not want the bats to live	91–100
under the bridge.	101–103

Name _____ Date _____

Oral Fluency Assessment

Unit 10, Nonfiction ▲

Read the following passage from *Houses on the Move* accurately and clearly in one minute.

Houses on the Move, pages 3–6

People live in many kinds of houses.	1–7
Some houses are big. Some houses are	8–14
small. They could be made of wood or	15–22
snow. Some people live in houses that stay	23–30
in one place. Other people live in houses	31–38
they can easily move.	39–42
One kind of shelter people can easily	43–49
move is a motor home. A motor home is	50–58
a house on wheels. People live in them	59–66
because they are easy to move.	67–72
Some people in the United States live	73–79
in motor homes. Their motor homes have	80–86
everything they need.	87–89
People who live in motor homes can	90–96
move whenever they want.	97–100

Scoring Oral Fluency Assessments

If the student reads the entire passage in one minute, use the appropriate Oral Reading Accuracy chart to identify the student's score.

Unit 10, Nonfiction ◆
Where Do Cats Live?
pages 3–11

Unit 10, Nonfiction ★
Bat Homes,
pages 3–7

Unit 10, Nonfiction ▲
Houses on the Move,
pages 3–6

Oral Reading Accuracy Number of Words = 102	
# of Errors	% Score
1	99
2	98
3	97
4	96
5	95
6	94
7	93
8	92
9	91
10	90

Oral Reading Accuracy Number of Words = 103	
# of Errors	% Score
1	99
2	98
3	97
4	96
5	95
6	94
7	93
8	92
9	91
10	90

Oral Reading Accuracy Number of Words = 100	
# of Errors	% Score
1	99
2	98
3	97
4	96
5	95
6	94
7	93
8	92
9	91
10	90

If the student does not read the entire passage, divide the Number of Correct Words Read Per Minute (WPM) by the Total Words Read to determine the student's score. Record these numbers on the Reading Rate and Accuracy chart.

Reading Rate and Accuracy	
Total Words Read:	_____
Number of Errors:	– _____
Number of Correct Words Read Per Minute (WPM):	_____
Accuracy Rate: (WPM ÷ Total Words Read)	_____